365 Insightful Questions for Girls Aged 13-14

365 Insightful Questions for Girls Aged 13-14

One Question a Day for Personal Growth and Confidence Building

Aria Capri Publishing
Devon Abbruzzese
Mauricio Vasquez

Toronto, Canada

365 Insightful Questions for Girls Aged 13-14 by Aria Capri Publishing [Aria Capri International Inc.]. All Rights Reserved.

All rights reserved. No part of this publication may be reproduced, distributed, shared with third parties, stored in any type of retrieval system, digitized, or transmitted in any form or by any means, including but not limited to electronic, mechanical, photocopying, recording, or otherwise, without the prior written permission of the publisher. Unauthorized reproduction or distribution of this publication, or any portion of it, may result in severe civil and criminal penalties and will be prosecuted to the fullest extent permitted by law.

Copyright © 2024, Aria Capri Publishing [Aria Capri International Inc.]. All Rights Reserved.

Authors:
Devon Abbruzzese
Mauricio Vasquez
Aria Capri Publishing

First Printing: May 2024

ISBN-978-1-998402-40-3 (Paperback book)
ISBN-978-1-998402-39-7 (Hardcover book)
ISBN-978-1-998402-38-0 (Electronic book)

Introduction

Welcome to a journey that begins with a question and unfolds into a myriad of discoveries about the world within and around us. This book is devoted to the early adolescent girls, those stepping into the formative years of ages 13 and 14, a period brimming with potential, curiosity, and profound transformation. It is during these years that young girls begin to navigate the complex pathways of identity formation, social relationships, and personal growth. This book, rooted in the practice of thoughtful inquiry, aims to guide them through these transformative years.

The art of questioning is not merely about seeking answers but about opening doors to new possibilities and perspectives. For early adolescents, questions can spark curiosity, drive learning, and encourage self-reflection. In a stage of life where everything is in flux—from their bodies to their sense of self—having a guide in the form of probing, insightful questions is invaluable.

The Importance of Engaging Early Adolescents with Thoughtful Questions

Early adolescence is a critical period for emotional and cognitive development. It is a time when young girls are forming their identities, questioning authority, and seeking to understand their place in the world. The questions we pose to them, therefore, should not only stimulate their minds but also respect their growing need for autonomy and inclusion.

Engaging young adolescents with meaningful questions serves multiple purposes:

- Self-Discovery: Well-crafted questions can help girls articulate their thoughts, explore their feelings, and clarify their values. Each question acts as a stepping stone toward deeper self-understanding and confidence.
- Learning and Cognitive Development: Questions that challenge their thinking can enhance cognitive skills such as critical thinking, problem-solving, and decision-making. These are essential skills that will benefit them throughout their lives.
- Emotional Intelligence: By encouraging them to reflect on their emotions and the emotions of others, we foster empathy and emotional regulation—key components of emotional intelligence.

- Strengthening Relationships: Thoughtful questions can also be a tool for parents, educators, and mentors to connect with young adolescents on a deeper level. This connection is pivotal as it provides the emotional security that girls need to explore and understand their rapidly changing world.

How Thoughtful Questions Can Transform Lives

The transition from childhood to adolescence brings with it a host of challenges and opportunities. In the realm of early adolescence, where peer influence begins to rival that of parental influence, it is crucial to establish open lines of communication. Thoughtful questions do more than just start a conversation; they build trust and open a dialogue that respects the adolescent's emerging independence.

Crafting the Questions

This book is structured to provide a question for each day of the year, designed to engage, inspire, and challenge. Each question has been carefully crafted to reflect the developmental needs of early adolescent girls, covering topics from self-esteem and body image to friendships and academic pressures. The questions encourage girls to look inward for answers and also to express their thoughts and feelings outwardly, thus practicing and strengthening their communication skills.

A Call to Engage

As we embark on this journey together, our goal is not only to provide answers but to ignite a passion for questioning, for it is through questions that we learn to live thoughtful, meaningful lives. This book is a tribute to the power of questions and their ability to transform the lives of young adolescent girls by helping them to know themselves better, to think critically about their world, and to connect deeply with others. Let us begin this journey with openness, readiness to explore, and the courage to ask that first, perhaps life-changing question.

Let the journey of questions begin.

Devon & Mauricio

Share Your Experience

Thank you for choosing this book. We hope this has provided meaningful insights and fostered valuable conversations for you and your child.

Your feedback helps us improve and helps other parents and young readers discover this resource. Reviews increase the book's visibility, making it easier for those who might benefit from its content to find it.

If you found this book helpful, please take a moment to leave a review by scanning this QR code.

Your experience can inspire and guide others on their journey of self-discovery and growth. We appreciate your support. Thank you.

Devon & Mauricio

Scan the QR code to access the full collection

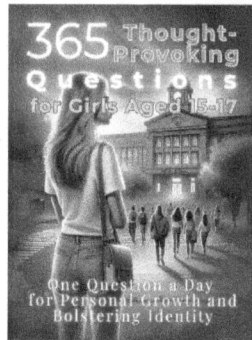

Guidelines for Asking Questions to Adolescents

Read the following guidelines to learn more about asking questions that unlock learning, foster communication and improve relationships.

- **Effective questions are open or focused, depending on the context**: Questions that open awareness and learning are open-ended questions that cannot be answered with a yes or no. Such questions evoke deeper thinking and reflection.
- **Effective questions support learning**: The goal is to stimulate thinking and deepen understanding of the situation. Insightful questions should focus attention on the most valuable aspects of the issue at hand, helping adolescents understand their experiences and feelings better.
- **Effective questions are asked for the benefit of others**: The intent is to stimulate the thinking and deepen the understanding of adolescents. It is not necessarily about the questioner and their needs.
- **Effective questions engage a personal response**: Engaging adolescents by inviting a personal response—how they feel, what emotions they are bringing to the situation—is crucial. The more a question invites a personal response to a challenge or choice, the more powerful it is for facilitating learning and growth.
- **Effective questions look beyond problems to future outcomes**: When adolescents are entangled in a problem, impactful questions shift the perspective from the problem to the solution, opening new opportunities for action and positive thinking.
- **Effective questions facilitate openness versus defensiveness**: Impactful questions are worded and expressed with a non-judgmental tone and open body language to prevent a defensive reaction. It is usually best to avoid questions that begin with "why" since they often elicit defensive responses or explanations.
- **Effective questions co-create best options versus manipulating outcomes**: Impactful questions are not intended to manipulate or lead adolescents to the option you might think is the best. If you want to suggest, it is best made directly as a suggestion versus a disguised directive through a question.
- **Less is more**: For questions, less is usually more. Ask only one question at a time and avoid long-winded, complicated questions.

<u>Disclaimer</u>

Dear Readers,

This book is designed to serve as a tool for personal growth, reflection, and exploring thoughts and feelings. The questions provided within these pages aim to inspire introspection and conversation, fostering a deeper understanding of oneself and the world.

However, it is important to understand that this book is not a substitute for professional advice, diagnosis, or treatment. While the questions can guide meaningful discussions and self-discovery, they are not intended to address or resolve serious issues or health concerns.

If you or your child encounters significant emotional, psychological, or physical challenges, we strongly recommend seeking the guidance of a qualified professional. This may include consulting a doctor, mental health professional, counselor, or any other relevant specialist who can provide the appropriate support and interventions.

The publisher, author, and any associated parties take no responsibility for any consequences resulting from the use of this book. It is up to the reader to exercise their judgment and discretion when engaging with the questions and interpreting their answers. The insights and reflections gained from this book should be seen as a starting point for further exploration and, when necessary, professional consultation.

We hope that this book serves as a valuable resource for personal growth and development. Remember, each individual's journey of self-discovery is unique, and seeking help when needed is a sign of strength and wisdom.

Day 1
How do you feel about the changes in your body as you grow? Do they make you excited, curious, or something else?

Day 2
What's one physical activity you enjoy that makes you feel strong and healthy?

Day 3
What is one thing you did today that made you feel proud of yourself?

Day 4
How do you handle situations when you feel upset or angry?

Day 5
Can you think of a time when you really understood how someone else was feeling? What was that like?

Day 6
Who is your closest friend right now, and what do you value most about your friendship?

Day 7
How do you feel about your family's expectations of you? Do they align with what you want for yourself?

Day 8
What's your favorite thing about using social media, and what's one thing you don't like about it?

Day 9
When solving a problem at school, what's your approach? Do you like to dive right in, ask for help, or think it over for a while?

Day 10
What book have you read recently that you enjoyed, and why?

Day 11
How do you prefer to study or learn new things—reading, watching videos, or doing activities?

Day 12
What's one thing you've learned in school that you found really interesting or surprising?

Day 13
Can you remember a dream you had recently? What happened, and how did it make you feel?

Day 14
What's one word you would use to describe your family, and why?

Day 15
If you could change one rule in your school, what would it be and why?

Day 16
What makes you feel stressed, and how do you usually cope with it?

Day 17
When you face a big challenge, who do you turn to for support, and why?

Day 18
Have you ever felt misunderstood by someone? How did you handle that situation?

Day 19
What's one aspect of your cultural background that you love and why?

Day 20
Do you think movies and TV shows influence how you think about the world? In what way?

Day 21
How does where you live (city, suburb, countryside) influence the activities you can do?

Day 22
What is one safety rule you always remember when you're online?

Day 23
When do you feel the most emotionally safe and supported? Who provides that feeling for you?

Day 24
What is one moral rule you think everyone should follow?

Day 25
Have your thoughts about what's right and wrong ever changed? What made them change?

Day 26
Do you have a place where you like to go when you need to think or relax? What is special about it?

Day 27
What's one way your life might be different if you lived in the opposite type of area (urban if rural, rural if urban)?

Day 28
What's one new food you tried recently? Did you like it? Why or why not?

Day 29
What is one goal you have for the next year?

Day 30
Can you think of a time when you helped someone else? What did you do, and how did it make you feel?

Day 31
When was the last time you learned a new skill? What was it, and how did you feel while learning it?

Day 32
How do you feel when you spend time away from screens? Do you find it easy or hard to disconnect?

Day 33
What are three words you would use to describe yourself, and why?

Day 34
What's the most comforting thing someone can say to you when you're upset?

Day 35
How do you decide if someone is trustworthy?

Day 36
What's one thing you wish teachers knew about what it's like to be a student today?

Day 37
How do you feel about group projects at school? Do you prefer working alone or with others?

Day 38
What's one memory that always makes you smile?

Day 39
When was the last time you tried something outside of your comfort zone?

Day 40
What do you appreciate most about your best friend?

Day 41
Do you ever feel pressure from social media to look or act a certain way? How do you handle it?

Day 42
What does 'family' mean to you?

Day 43
What's your favorite way to relax after a long day?

Day 44
If you could invent something that would make life easier for people, what would it be?

<u>Day 45</u>
How do you like to celebrate your achievements?

<u>Day 46</u>
What's one personal challenge you've overcome this year?

<u>Day 47</u>
How does it feel to grow up in your particular culture? What are the best and most challenging parts?

<u>Day 48</u>
What role does music play in your life?

Day 49
How important is it for you to have a quiet space to study?

Day 50
What's your favorite subject in school, and what makes it your favorite?

Day 51
What's one new thing you would like to try this school year?

Day 52
Who in your life makes you feel the most supported?

Day 53
What is your favorite way to express your creativity?

Day 54
What do you think makes a person a good listener?

Day 55
How do you feel about asking for help when you need it?

Day 56
What are some ways you can show kindness to others?

Day 57
How do you deal with disagreements with your friends?

Day 58
What are your thoughts on the importance of physical exercise?

Day 59
How do you feel right before a test at school?

Day 60
What's one thing you love about your home?

Day 61
What do you think is the biggest challenge facing your generation?

Day 62
How do you approach making new friends?

Day 63
What are your strategies for coping with anxiety or stress?

Day 64
What does being independent mean to you?

Day 65
How do you feel about the way you are portrayed in the media?

Day 66
What's one thing you wish adults understood better about kids your age?

Day 67
What role does technology play in your daily life?

Day 68
How do you feel about your future?

Day 69
What's one world issue that you feel strongly about?

Day 70
How do you approach homework and assignments?

Day 71
What's one hobby that you really enjoy?

Day 72
How do you handle conflicts within your family?

Day 73
What's your favorite outdoor activity?

Day 74
What are some ways you take care of your mental health?

Day 75
How do you celebrate your cultural or family traditions?

Day 76
What's the most important lesson you've learned from a friend?

Day 77

What's your favorite thing to do on weekends?

Day 78

How do you like to prepare for school exams?

Day 79

What's one thing that makes you unique from your friends?

Day 80

How do you feel about sharing your feelings with others?

Day 81
When was the last time you learned something new from a friend?

Day 82
What's your favorite way to unwind after a stressful day?

Day 83
How do you feel about the environment and your role in protecting it?

Day 84
If you could improve one thing about your school, what would it be?

Day 85
What's one piece of advice you would give to your younger self?

Day 86
What does a perfect day look like to you?

Day 87
What are your thoughts on equality and fairness at school or in sports?

Day 88
How do you handle feelings of jealousy or competitiveness?

Day 89
What's something you're looking forward to in the next month?

Day 90
Do you prefer to lead or follow in group activities? Why?

Day 91
How do you express gratitude towards others?

Day 92
What's one way you've changed in the past year?

<u>Day 93</u>
How do you prepare for a big presentation or performance?

<u>Day 94</u>
What's one thing that scares you, and how do you deal with your fear?

<u>Day 95</u>
How important is it for you to have time alone?

<u>Day 96</u>
What are your thoughts on honesty? Is it always best to be honest?

<u>Day 97</u>
How do you decide what is right and wrong?

<u>Day 98</u>
What's one way you've helped your community or school?

<u>Day 99</u>
Who is your role model, and what qualities do they have that you admire?

<u>Day 100</u>
What's one skill you'd like to develop or improve?

Day 101
How do you react when things don't go as planned?

Day 102
What does courage mean to you?

Day 103
How do you deal with peer pressure?

Day 104
What are your aspirations for the future?

Day 105
What's one positive change you'd like to make in your life?

Day 106
How do you handle criticism or feedback?

Day 107
What's your approach to managing your time, especially with schoolwork and hobbies?

Day 108
What's one act of kindness you've witnessed or performed recently?

<u>Day 109</u>
How do you feel about your responsibilities at home?

<u>Day 110</u>
What's one thing you admire about your parents or guardians?

<u>Day 111</u>
How do you feel when you help others?

<u>Day 112</u>
What's one challenge you've faced in dealing with your emotions?

<u>Day 113</u>
What's your favorite memory from the past year?

<u>Day 114</u>
How do you think others perceive you, and how does that make you feel?

<u>Day 115</u>
What's one goal you have for the next school year?

<u>Day 116</u>
How do you balance your personal interests with school demands?

Day 117
What's one new activity or club you'd like to join?

Day 118
How do you feel about your personal safety in public places?

Day 119
What's one personal belief that is important to you?

Day 120
How do you cope with feelings of loneliness or isolation?

Day 121

What's your favorite family tradition and why?

Day 122

How do you approach solving a difficult math problem or project?

Day 123

What's one thing that makes you feel confident?

Day 124

How do you handle a disagreement with a friend?

Day 125

What's one way you've grown in your understanding of other cultures?

Day 126

If you could travel anywhere, where would you go and why?

Day 127

What's one book that has had a significant impact on you?

Day 128

How do you feel about the role of technology in your education?

Day 129
What's your strategy for dealing with a busy week of school and extracurricular activities?

Day 130
What's the most important quality you look for in a friend?

Day 131
How do you deal with feeling overwhelmed by school or other commitments?

Day 132
What's one way you show your family you love them?

Day 133
How do you feel when you achieve something you worked hard for?

Day 134
What's your favorite subject in school, and what do you like about it?

Day 135
What's one way you've helped someone in your community?

Day 136
How do you relax after a long day?

<u>Day 137</u>
What's something you admire about your teachers?

<u>Day 138</u>
What's a recent challenge you overcame?

<u>Day 139</u>
How do you feel about your privacy online?

<u>Day 140</u>
What's one way you could make a positive impact on your school?

Day 141
How do you feel about the pressures to succeed academically?

Day 142
What's your favorite way to spend time outdoors?

Day 143
How do you think being a teenager today is different from when your parents were teens?

Day 144
What's one thing you're grateful for today?

Day 145
How do you express yourself creatively?

Day 146
What's one life skill you'd like to learn this year?

Day 147
How do you handle situations where you feel excluded?

Day 148
What's your favorite way to celebrate your achievements?

Day 149

How do you manage your responsibilities at home and school?

Day 150

What's one thing you would change about your school environment?

Day 151

What's one lesson you've learned from a mistake you made?

Day 152

How do you feel about your future career possibilities?

Day 153

What's one aspect of your personality that you're proud of?

Day 154

How do you react when someone disagrees with you in a discussion?

Day 155

What's your favorite way to learn something new?

Day 156

How do you stay motivated when you have a big project?

Day 157
What's one act of kindness you observed this week?

Day 158
How do you define success for yourself?

Day 159
What's one change you'd like to see in the world?

Day 160
How do you balance your time between friends and family?

Day 161
What's your strategy for dealing with distractions while studying?

Day 162
How do you deal with nerves before a test or presentation?

Day 163
What's one thing you do to help protect the environment?

Day 164
Who is someone in your life who inspires you and why?

Day 165
What's your favorite sport or physical activity, and what do you enjoy about it?

Day 166
How do you feel about the advice you receive from older family members?

Day 167
What's one goal you have for improving your physical health?

Day 168
How do you approach making new friends at school?

Day 169

What's your favorite memory from this school year?

Day 170

How do you feel about your responsibilities at home?

Day 171

What's something new you'd like to learn outside of school?

Day 172

How do you handle feelings of sadness or disappointment?

Day 173
What's one way you've shown resilience in a tough situation?

Day 174
How do you like to celebrate special occasions with your friends?

Day 175
What's something creative you've done recently?

Day 176
How do you manage stress from school or extracurricular activities?

<u>Day 177</u>
What's one positive change you've noticed about yourself this year?

<u>Day 178</u>
How do you decide what's fair in a disagreement?

<u>Day 179</u>
What's your approach to learning a new skill or hobby?

<u>Day 180</u>
How do you prepare for a school exam or project?

Day 181
What's one piece of technology you find invaluable for your studies?

Day 182
How do you handle social situations that you find uncomfortable?

Day 183
What's one way you've contributed to a group or team effort?

Day 184
What do you do to ensure your own online safety?

Day 185
How do you express gratitude to someone who has helped you?

Day 186
What's one thing you'd like to improve about your communication skills?

Day 187
What's one cultural event or tradition you particularly enjoy?

Day 188
How do you make decisions about spending and saving money?

<u>Day 189</u>
What's a recent situation where you had to be brave?

<u>Day 190</u>
How do you prioritize your homework and leisure activities?

<u>Day 191</u>
What's one thing you admire about a community leader in your area?

<u>Day 192</u>
How do you feel when you try to navigate a conflict among friends?

Day 193

What's your favorite way to start the day, and how does it set the tone for you?

Day 194

Who in your life do you talk to when you need advice?

Day 195

What's one thing you've learned about managing time effectively?

Day 196

How do you approach a task you find uninteresting or difficult?

Day 197
What's something new you discovered about yourself this month?

Day 198
How do you celebrate your cultural heritage?

Day 199
What's a hobby you'd like to explore more?

Day 200
How do you handle it when you and a friend have a misunderstanding?

Day 201
What inspires you to learn?

Day 202
How do you take care of your mental health during stressful times?

Day 203
What's your strategy for dealing with change?

Day 204
How do you decide what's important to share online?

Day 205
What's one way you've shown independence this year?

Day 206
How do you like to receive feedback?

Day 207
What's a book that influenced your thinking?

Day 208
How do you deal with the pressure of expectations from others?

<u>Day 209</u>
What's something you do to improve your mood when you're feeling down?

<u>Day 210</u>
How do you decide who to trust?

<u>Day 211</u>
What's a goal you have for your personal growth?

<u>Day 212</u>
How do you feel about public speaking?

Day 213
What's a subject you wish was taught at school?

Day 214
How do you maintain friendships with people who have different interests?

Day 215
What's one way you try to make a positive impact on your community?

Day 216
How do you prepare for a big event or exam?

Day 217

What's one way you have found to balance school and personal life?

Day 218

How do you approach solving a problem with someone else?

Day 219

What's one thing you enjoy about the place you live?

Day 220

How do you handle peer pressure in school?

<u>Day 221</u>
What's something you've learned from a mistake this year?

<u>Day 222</u>
How do you keep yourself organized with school assignments and deadlines?

<u>Day 223</u>
What's one new skill or hobby you're interested in trying next year?

<u>Day 224</u>
How do you react when someone compliments you?

Day 225
What's one thing you've done recently that took courage?

Day 226
How do you deal with feeling overwhelmed?

Day 227
What's an important lesson you've learned from a family member?

Day 228
How do you choose what extracurricular activities to participate in?

Day 229
What's something you feel passionate about?

Day 230
How do you think you've changed in the past year?

Day 231
What's one area of your life where you feel you've made significant improvement?

Day 232
Who is a person in your life that makes you feel understood?

Day 233

What's a tradition you love participating in with your friends or family?

Day 234

How do you express yourself when you feel happy?

Day 235

What's a skill you would like to master over the next few years?

Day 236

What's something that you're curious about right now?

Day 237
How do you approach learning about topics that challenge your beliefs?

Day 238
What's one way you've contributed to making your school or community better?

Day 239
How do you feel about the role of technology in relationships?

Day 240
What's one piece of advice you would give to someone younger than you?

<u>Day 241</u>
How do you decide if you need to stick with something difficult or let it go?

<u>Day 242</u>
What's one thing you do to stay focused when you're studying?

<u>Day 243</u>
How do you celebrate personal successes?

<u>Day 244</u>
What's one life lesson you've learned from someone in your life?

Day 245
How do you cope with feelings of uncertainty about the future?

Day 246
What's one thing you would like to change about your daily routine?

Day 247
How do you respond to challenges or setbacks?

Day 248
What's a recent positive experience that has impacted you deeply?

Day 249
What's one thing you appreciate about your cultural background?

Day 250
How do you handle disagreements with someone you care about?

Day 251
What's one topic you feel very knowledgeable about?

Day 252
How do you maintain your personal values when pressured by peers?

Day 253
What's one dream you hope to achieve in the next five years?

Day 254
How do you balance your personal needs with the needs of others?

Day 255
What's one way you practice self-care?

Day 256
How do you handle feeling left out or excluded?

Day 257
What's one activity that always makes you lose track of time?

Day 258
How do you approach making new friends?

Day 259
What's one subject or activity you wish you knew more about?

Day 260
How do you deal with the stress of school exams?

Day 261
What's one thing you wish people knew about you?

Day 262
How do you celebrate your friendships?

Day 263
What's one personal strength you rely on in difficult times?

Day 264
How do you approach decision-making?

<u>Day 265</u>
What's a book or movie that has inspired you recently?

<u>Day 266</u>
How do you prioritize your mental health?

<u>Day 267</u>
What's one area where you seek to grow or improve?

<u>Day 268</u>
How do you manage your time between school, hobbies, and relaxation?

Day 269
What's one thing you've learned about yourself through a challenging experience?

Day 270
How do you encourage yourself when you're feeling down?

Day 271
What's one thing you've done recently that you never thought you could do?

Day 272
How do you feel when you work on a team?

<u>Day 273</u>
What's one way you'd like to change the world?

<u>Day 274</u>
How do you deal with a day that doesn't go as planned?

<u>Day 275</u>
What are you most passionate about learning right now?

<u>Day 276</u>
What's something you've learned from a friend that was surprising?

Day 277
How do you express love and appreciation to those around you?

Day 278
What's one habit you're proud of developing?

Day 279
How do you find balance between school and your hobbies?

Day 280
What's the most useful piece of advice you've ever received?

Day 281

How do you respond when someone challenges your beliefs?

Day 282

What's one thing you would like to learn that isn't taught in school?

Day 283

How do you approach a problem that seems unsolvable?

Day 284

What's one way you show kindness to others?

Day 285
How do you celebrate your achievements?

Day 286
What's a recent dream you remember that made an impression on you?

Day 287
How do you handle situations where you feel out of your depth?

Day 288
What's something that motivates you every day?

Day 289
How do you prioritize your tasks when you have a lot to do?

Day 290
What's one thing you admire about your parents or guardians?

Day 291
How do you maintain your focus during long assignments?

Day 292
What's one personal goal you have for the next month?

Day 293
How do you approach learning from your mistakes?

Day 294
What's one way you've grown in your understanding of others?

Day 295
How do you deal with feelings of impatience or frustration?

Day 296
What's one thing you're looking forward to learning?

Day 29
How do you stay motivated when progress seems slow?

Day 298
What's one way you could help someone else today?

Day 299
What's a trait you admire in others and why?

Day 300
How do you handle unexpected changes?

Day 301
What's something you've done that you initially resisted but ended up enjoying?

Day 302
What's one thing you're grateful for in your community?

Day 303
How do you handle the pressure of expectations from yourself and others?

Day 304
What's something that makes you feel confident?

Day 305
How do you handle days when you feel low?

Day 306
What's one area of your life where you've seen significant improvement?

Day 307
How do you decide when to ask for help?

Day 308
What's one way you plan to contribute to your school or community?

Day 309
What's something new you've discovered about yourself this year?

Day 310
How do you deal with setbacks?

Day 311
What's one subject or skill you'd like to learn more about?

Day 312
What's one way you take care of your physical health?

Day 313

How do you express creativity?

Day 314

What's one thing you would like to achieve by the end of this year?

Day 315

How do you handle criticism?

Day 316

What's something you've learned about relationships this year?

Day 317
What's one way you stay organized?

Day 318
How do you deal with conflicts with friends?

Day 319
What's one new activity or hobby you'd like to try?

Day 320
What's one thing that inspires you?

Day 321

How do you handle nervousness before a big event?

Day 322

What's one personal challenge you would like to overcome?

Day 323

How do you manage stress in your daily life?

Day 324

What's one thing you do to help others in your community?

Day 325
How do you balance your personal interests with academic responsibilities?

Day 326
What's one new thing you'd like to try in the new year?

Day 327
What's one lesson you've learned from a challenging experience?

Day 328
How do you deal with disappointment?

Day 329
What's one way you relax after a busy week?

Day 330
How do you approach making decisions about your future?

Day 331
What's one thing you've done to improve your local environment?

Day 332
How do you handle feeling under pressure?

Day 333
What's one thing you would like to learn about other cultures?

Day 334
How do you maintain motivation for a long-term project?

Day 335
What's something you've done that made you feel incredibly proud?

Day 336
How do you approach difficult conversations?

Day 337
What's one area where you'd like to see change in your school?

Day 338
What's one way you try to understand people who are different from you?

Day 339
How do you plan your day to ensure you accomplish your goals?

Day 340
What's one way you've contributed to a team or group effort?

Day 341
How do you prepare for an important test or assessment?

Day 342
What's something you do to show someone you care?

Day 343
How do you deal with feeling overwhelmed by responsibilities?

Day 344
What's one thing you'd like to change about your daily habits?

<u>Day 345</u>
How do you stay connected with friends?

<u>Day 346</u>
What's one way you cope with stress?

<u>Day 347</u>
How do you approach learning a new subject or skill?

<u>Day 348</u>
What's something you've achieved that you never thought possible?

Day 349
How do you manage your time when you have multiple tasks?

Day 350
What's one thing you would change about the way you communicate?

Day 351
How do you handle distractions when you need to focus?

Day 352
What's one way you show appreciation for your family?

Day 353

How do you handle situations where you feel you've been treated unfairly?

Day 354

What's one positive impact you hope to have on those around you?

Day 355

How do you approach setting and achieving personal goals?

Day 356

What's one way you stay active and healthy?

Day 357

How do you handle moments of self-doubt?

Day 358

What's something you appreciate about your education?

Day 359

How do you handle feelings of sadness or loneliness?

Day 360

What's one lesson you've learned from a book or movie recently?

<u>Day 361</u>
How do you make decisions about using social media?

<u>Day 362</u>
What's one way you've grown in your understanding of yourself?

<u>Day 363</u>
How do you prepare for new challenges?

<u>Day 364</u>
What's something you do to maintain your mental health?

Day 365
Reflecting on the past year, what has been the most important lesson you've learned about yourself?

Share Your Experience

Thank you for choosing this book. We hope this has provided meaningful insights and fostered valuable conversations for you and your child.

Your feedback helps us improve and helps other parents and young readers discover this resource. Reviews increase the book's visibility, making it easier for those who might benefit from its content to find it.

If you found this book helpful, please take a moment to leave a review by scanning this QR code.

Your experience can inspire and guide others on their journey of self-discovery and growth. We appreciate your support. Thank you.

Devon & Mauricio